Children's Rosary®

A Prayer Group Movement for Children

By
Blythe Marie Kaufman DMD MDS

Illustrations by
Cecil Kornreich, Alina Kaufman and Angie Quintero

Preface by
Most Reverend Henry J. Mansell
Archbishop of Hartford, CT USA

Children's Rosary

A Prayer Group Movement for Children

Preface

"This booklet provides a wonderful guide to a richer and deeper understanding of the Most Holy Rosary of the Blessed Virgin Mary. It is clear that this booklet does not offer a new Rosary, but rather serves to assist the children who pray the Rosary to do so in a special way bringing them to safety and holiness of life under the intercession and protection of the Blessed Mother. May the mysteries of the Rosary and the intercession of the Blessed Mother draw those who pray the Rosary closer to Our Lord."

Most Reverend Henry J. Mansell
Archbishop of Hartford, CT USA

Introduction

In a homily given by Pope Benedict XVI on October 11, 2012 the Holy Father ushered in a "New Evangelization" and went on to say "recent decades have seen the advance of a spiritual desertification." We see every day around us "what a life or a world without God looks like." The Holy Father invoked hope when he proclaimed: "In the desert people of faith are needed who, with their own lives point out the way to the Promised Land and keep hope alive. Living faith opens the heart to the grace of God which frees us from pessimism."

How do we do this? How do we through our own lives point the way to the Promised Land?

Pope Benedict goes on in his homily to provide such help for us, "May the Virgin Mary always shine out as a star along the way of the New Evangelization. May she help us to put into practice the Apostle Paul's exhortation, 'Let the word of Christ dwell in you richly, teach and admonish one another in all wisdom [...] And whatever you do, in word or deed, do everything in the name of the Lord Jesus, giving thanks to God the Father through Him.'" (*Col* 3:16-17) Amen.

Amidst this religious desert which Pope Benedict describes, our children stand in the middle surrounded by secularism and consumerism, drowning in a Godless culture. The Children's Rosary is intended to be a life line to our young people who represent the heart of the Church and the heart of the family. By means of the Holy Rosary our children will be guided to safety and holiness under the protection of Our Blessed Mother.

The Power of the Rosary
How will the rosary sanctify our children? Pope John Paul II describes how this sanctification can occur in the *Rosarium Virginis Mariae* when he quotes Blessed Bartolo Longo: "Just as two friends, frequently in each other's company, tend to develop similar habits, so too, by holding familiar converse with Jesus and the Blessed Virgin, by meditating on the mysteries of the Rosary and by living the same life in Holy Communion, we can become, to the extent of our lowliness, similar to

them and can learn from these supreme models a life of humility, poverty, hiddenness, patience and perfection."

The *Catechism of the Catholic Church* also recognizes the importance of the Holy Rosary as an "epitome of the whole Gospel."(*Catechism* 971)

Our Blessed Mother a Place of Refuge
Our Blessed Mother is always pointing to her Son. She wants none of the glory for herself. Instead she means to take our hands and bring us on the straightest path to her Son. Her last recorded words in Scripture were at the wedding feast of Cana when she said, "Do whatever He tells you." (*Jn* 2:5 NAB)

Our Lord means to help us by giving us His own Mother who nurtured and held Him as a child and then held Him after his final sacrifice for us on the cross. Our Lady always has her arms outstretched to her children...calling them to herself and through her intercession to the loving heart of her Son, Jesus.

"Before, by yourself, you couldn't. Now, you've turned to Our Lady, and with her, how easy!"(St. Josemaria Escriva)

Our Lord has chosen His Mother as a "mystical channel, His aqueduct, through which He causes His mercies to flow gently and abundantly." (Saint Louis Marie de Montfort in the Treatise on *True Devotion to the Blessed Virgin*)

The *Catechism of the Catholic Church* also recognizes "the Blessed Virgin as Mother of God to whose protection the faithful fly in all their dangers and needs" and acknowledges "devotion to the Blessed Virgin is intrinsic to Christian worship."(*Catechism* 971)

If one worries about affording Mary too much honor Saint Louis Marie de Montfort states: "We never give more honor to Jesus than when we honor His Mother, and we honor her simply and solely to honor Him all the more perfectly. We go to her only as a way leading to the goal we seek - Jesus, her Son." Saint Maximilian Kolbe echoes this sentiment,

"Never be afraid of loving the Blessed Virgin too much. You can never love her more than Jesus did."

The Role Children Will Play in Our Church
"Amen, I say to you, unless you turn and become like children, you will not enter the kingdom of heaven." (*Mt* 18:3 NAB) This was part of the Gospel reading on the Memorial of Our Lady of the Rosary on October 7th, 2012. If we reflect on these words of Jesus one might question why children have not played a larger role in our Church in the past. While prayer groups exist in many parishes for adults there is a scarcity of such groups designed for children.

If we still ask whether Our Lord intended our children to meet Him in prayer, we have only to return to Scripture: "When Jesus saw this He became indignant and said to them, 'Let the children come to me; do not prevent them, for the Kingdom of God belongs to such as these. Amen, I say to you, whoever does not receive the Kingdom of God like a child will not enter it.'" (*Mk* 10: 14-15 NAB)

Our Blessed Mother has chosen to convey messages to the world and the importance of the Holy Rosary through children such as the three children of Fatima. Our Lady also appeared to the child, Bernadette, at Lourdes France while she was praying the Rosary. If Our Lord and His Mother have been so clear about the importance of children praying and leading prayer, might we listen to their words and example and bring our children to them?

Through the means of the Children's Rosary our children will experience prayer with other children under the watchful eye of their Heavenly Mother. They will be schooled in virtue and holiness by the most perfect of teachers: Our Blessed Mother. Jesus has told us something else about our children in the portion of St. Matthew's Gospel: "I give praise to you, Father, Lord of heaven and earth, for although you have hidden these things from the wise and the learned you have revealed them to the childlike."(*Mt* 11:25 NAB)

Our children have an enormous capacity for spirituality and a deep relationship with Our Lord and His Mother. In this springtime of faith may we look to the future of our Church, our children, to help lead us all back to the warm embrace of Our Savior.

The Role of Parents
"Through the grace of the sacrament of marriage, parents receive the responsibility and privilege of evangelizing their children." (*Catechism* 2225) When should this evangelization begin? The catechism is clear that it should start at an early age: "Parents should initiate their children at an early age into the mysteries of the faith of which they are the 'first heralds' for their children. They should associate them from their tenderest years with the life of the Church." (*Catechism* 2225)

The Children's Rosary is a means for parents to expose their children to prayer at an early age and develop a faith steeped in the Tradition of the Catholic Church.

What is the Children's Rosary?
The Children's Rosary is a lay prayer movement for children. It is an effort to begin in parishes rosary prayer groups composed of children and led by children. The target age of the children for these prayer groups is between 4 and 14 years old.

The children of Fatima and Bernadette of Lourdes were all within this age range. However, there is flexibility at each end of the range and children should never be turned away if they have a desire to be part of a prayer group.

Of special note are children with disabilities who may be older in age but have a special place in the Children's Rosary. These children should be encouraged to be a part of this prayer movement. Adults are always welcome and encouraged to come to the Children's Rosary. These individuals are the special "guardian angels" of this movement.

Through prayer of the Rosary Our Lady will guide our young people while at the same time sanctify families and Parishes.

How the Children's Rosary Began

The Children's Rosary began out of love for Our Lady and her Son, Jesus. It was born out of a call for help. The request for help came from our pastor who saw his Parish suffering a financial crisis and worried for its future existence. In prayerful reflection on this call for help an inspiration came to bring our children before Our Lady and Our Lord in the prayer of the rosary, for we know how strong and dear are the prayers of children and how all heaven delights in them.

The first meeting of the Children's Rosary was on April 10, 2011. It was the Sunday before Palm Sunday that year. A group of children gathered that morning. The children knelt before a statue of Our Lady and prayed as a group for our parish and the intentions of Our Lady. The weekend of the first Children's Rosary had a record collection surpassed only by Easter and Christmas for the remainder of the year. There was nothing special about that weekend except for a small group of children who knelt in prayer of the Holy Rosary.

The Children's Rosary has been dedicated to the Sacred Heart of Jesus and Immaculate Heart of Mary. It is therefore under the protection and guidance of Christ and His Mother.

The children finish each Children's Rosary with an Our Father, Hail Mary, and Glory Be, for Our Holy Father the Pope. It is our hope that the Children's Rosary will be a strong source of prayers and blessings for the Holy Father, our Church as a whole, and the New Evangelization called upon by Pope Benedict XVI.

The Children's Rosary which once began in one Parish has now grown and by the grace of God will continue to grow so that Children's Rosary groups will exist in parishes across the globe.

How to Begin a Children's Rosary

If there isn't a Children's Rosary near you consider starting one. Our Lady has continued to show us through the apparitions in Lourdes and Fatima that she is calling our children to prayer, and in a special way, the Rosary.

Steps to Begin a Children's Rosary in Your Parish
1) Obtain permission from your pastor to begin a Children's Rosary group.
2) Choose a location (usually in a church or parish center but does not have to be limited to those locations).
3) Choose a regular meeting time (monthly or if interest exists, weekly).
4) Invite a small group of families and children to your first Children's Rosary and consider putting a notice in your church bulletin.
5) Register your Children's Rosary at www.childrensrosary.org or mail to Children's Rosary, P.O. Box 271743, West Hartford, CT 06127 USA (In this way we will have a central list of all Children's Rosary groups formed and those looking for a Children's Rosary will easily be able to find one on www.childrensrosary.org).

Guidelines for Your First Children's Rosary
1) Begin by consecrating your new group to the Sacred Heart of Jesus and Immaculate Heart of Mary.
2) Bring the children together in front of those gathered and have them kneel (pillows are a welcome addition for them to kneel on).
3) In turns have a child stand and lead a decade of the rosary (if a microphone is present this is a nice way for their soft voices to be heard).
4) The child should say the first part of each prayer:
Hail Mary, full of grace.
the Lord is with thee.
Blessed art thou among women,
and blessed is the fruit of thy womb, Jesus.

The entire group then responds together:
Holy Mary, Mother of God,
pray for us sinners,
now and at the hour of our death. Amen.
A similar alternating arrangement should be used for the Our Father and Glory Be.
5) An optional addition is the use of flowers (roses or any other

flower). This is particularly nice for smaller children not able to lead or children with disabilities preventing them from leading. At the end of each decade a child is asked to place a flower at the foot of a statue of Mary if available (otherwise just place the roses in a small pile on the ground in front of where the children are praying). While the child is placing the flower an adult is saying, "Mary we humbly place this flower at your feet and ask for the gift of... Faith" if one were saying the first glorious mystery. The gifts asked for correspond to the fruits of the mysteries.

6) Consider having a prayer book with illustrations of the mysteries of the rosary for the children to use during prayer. (The Children's Rosary book was designed for this purpose but any visual aid can be used).

7) Consider having a petition box. The children can decorate the box if desired and it can be placed in front of the children while they are saying their monthly rosary. If the group desires and is given permission from the pastor the box can be left out for members of the parish to place petitions in all month.

Prayers of the Rosary

Sign of the Cross
In the name of the Father, and of the Son, and of the Holy Spirit. Amen. (As you say this, with your right hand touch your forehead when you say Father, touch your breastbone when you say Son, touch your left shoulder when you say Holy, and touch your right shoulder when you say Spirit.)

The Apostles' Creed
I believe in God, the Father Almighty,
Creator of Heaven and earth; and in Jesus Christ,
His only Son Our Lord, Who was conceived by the Holy Spirit,
born of the Virgin Mary, suffered under Pontius Pilate, was crucified, died, and was buried.
He descended into Hell; the third day He rose again from the dead;
He ascended into Heaven, and sitteth at the right hand of God, the Father almighty; from thence He shall come to judge the living and the dead.

I believe in the Holy Spirit, the holy Catholic Church, the communion of saints, the forgiveness of sins, the resurrection of the body and life everlasting. Amen.

The Our Father
Our Father, Who art in heaven, hallowed be Thy Name. Thy Kingdom come. Thy Will be done, on earth as it is in Heaven. Give us this day our daily bread. And forgive us our trespasses, as we forgive those who trespass against us. And lead us not into temptation, but deliver us from evil. Amen.

The Hail Mary
Hail Mary, full of grace, the Lord is with thee; blessed art thou among women, and blessed is the fruit of thy womb, Jesus. Holy Mary, Mother of God, pray for us sinners, now and at the hour of death. Amen.

Glory be to the Father
Glory Be to the Father, and to the Son, and to the Holy Spirit. As it was in the beginning, is now and will be forever. Amen.

The Hail! Holy Queen
Hail! Holy Queen, Mother of mercy; our life, our sweetness, and our hope. To thee do we cry, poor banished children of Eve. To thee do we send up our sighs, mourning and weeping in this vale of tears. Turn, then, most gracious advocate, thine eyes of mercy toward us. And after this, our exile, show unto us the blessed fruit of thy womb, Jesus. O clement, O loving, O sweet Virgin Mary. Pray for us, O holy Mother of God, that we may be made worthy of the promises of Christ. Amen.

Mysteries of the Rosary with the Fruits

Disposition should be one of contemplation and reflection. Pope John Paul II in the *Rosarium Virginis Mariae* describes the Rosary as "an exquisitely contemplative prayer. Without this contemplative dimension, it would lose its meaning."

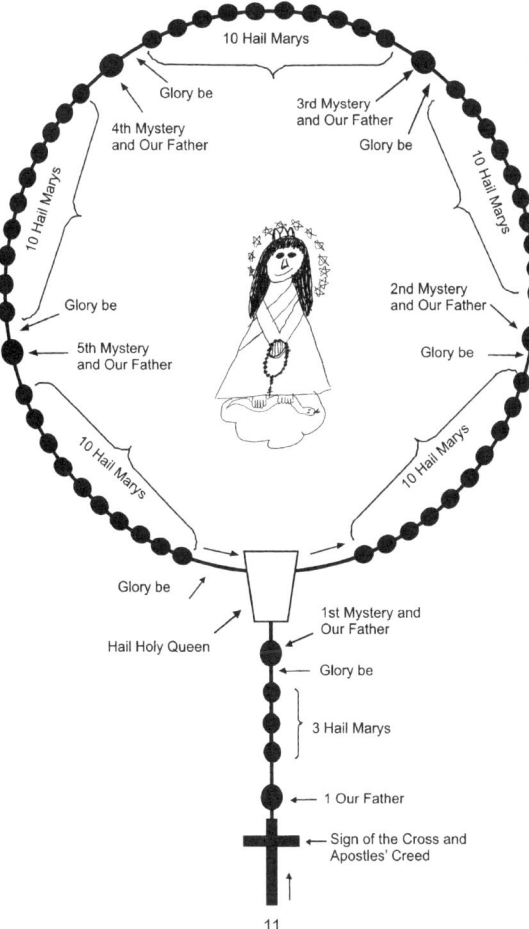

11

On Monday and Saturday, meditate on the "Joyful Mysteries"

First Decade: The Annunciation of Gabriel to Mary (*Lk* 1:26-38)

FRUIT: HUMILITY

Thinking of ...
Joy radiating from the event,[1] when Gabriel greets the Virgin Mary "Hail, favored one! The Lord is with you." (*Lk* 1:28 NAB) Mary humbly responds, "Behold I am the handmaid of the Lord. May it be done to me according to your word." (*Lk* 1:38 NAB)

Second Decade: The Visitation of Mary to Elizabeth (*Lk* 1:39-56)

FRUIT: LOVE OF NEIGHBOR

Thinking of ...
Exultation when Mary sees Elizabeth and the sound of Mary's voice and the presence of Christ in her womb cause John to "leap for joy." (cf. *Lk* 1:44)[1]

Third Decade: The Birth of Our Lord (*Lk* 2:1-21)

FRUIT: POVERTY

Thinking of ...
Gladness[1] as the baby Jesus is born and placed in "swaddling clothes." (cf. *Lk* 2:7)

Fourth Decade: The Presentation of Our Lord (*Lk* 2:22-38)

FRUIT: OBEDIENCE

Thinking of ...
The joy of the Child's consecration in the Temple[1] as a result of the obedience of Mary and Joseph to the law of God.

15

Fifth Decade: The Finding of Our Lord in the Temple (*Lk* 2:41-52)

FRUIT: JOY IN FINDING JESUS

Thinking of ...
Joy mixed with drama as Mary and Joseph find twelve-year-old Jesus in the Temple.[1]

On Thursday, meditate on the "Luminous Mysteries"

First Decade: The Baptism of Our Lord in the River Jordan (*Mt* 3:13-17)

FRUIT: OPENNESS TO THE HOLY SPIRIT

Thinking of ...
The heavens open wide and the voice of the Father declares Him the beloved Son (cf. *Mt* 3:17 and parallels), while the Spirit descends on Him to invest Him with the mission which He is to carry out.[1]

Second Decade: The Wedding at Cana, when Christ manifested Himself (*Jn* 2:1-11)

FRUIT: TO JESUS THROUGH MARY

Thinking of ...
When Christ changes water into wine and opens the hearts of the disciples to faith, thanks to the intervention of Mary.[1]

Third Decade: The Proclamation of the Kingdom of God (*Mk* 1:14-15)

FRUIT: REPENTANCE AND TRUST IN GOD

Thinking of ...
Jesus proclaims the coming of the Kingdom of God while forgiving the sins of all who draw near to Him in humble trust. (cf. *Mk* 2:3-13; *Lk* 7:47-48)[1]

Fourth Decade: The Transfiguration of Our Lord (*Mt* 17:1-8)

FRUIT: DESIRE FOR HOLINESS

Thinking of ...
The Glory of the Godhead which shines forth from the face of Christ as the Father commands the astonished Apostles to "listen to Him." (cf. *Lk* 9:35 and parallels)[1]

Fifth Decade: The Last Supper, when Our Lord gave us the Holy Eucharist (*Mt* 26: 26-30)

FRUIT: ADORATION

Thinking of ...
Christ offers His body and blood as food under the signs of bread and wine and testifies "to the end" His love for humanity. (*Jn* 13:1 NAB)[1]

On Tuesday and Friday, meditate on the "Sorrowful Mysteries"

First Decade: The Agony of Our Lord in the Garden (*Mt* 26:36-56)

FRUIT: SORROW FOR OUR SINS

Thinking of ...
In the garden of Gethsemane, Jesus encounters all the temptations and confronts all the sins of humanity, in order to say to the Father: "Not My will but Yours be done."(*Lk* 22:42 and parallels)[1]

Second Decade: Our Lord is Scourged at the Pillar (*Mt* 27:26)

FRUIT: PURITY

Thinking of ...
How the Son of God humbled Himself out of love.[1]

Third Decade: Our Lord is Crowned with Thorns (*Mt* 27:27-31)

FRUIT: COURAGE

Thinking of ...
"Weaving a crown out of thorns, they placed it on His head, and a reed in His right hand. And kneeling before Him they mocked Him." (*Mt* 27:29 NAB)

Fourth Decade: Our Lord Carries the Cross to Calvary (*Mt* 27:32)

FRUIT: PATIENCE

Thinking of ...
Jesus carrying the heavy cross according to the Father's will.[1]

Fifth Decade: The Crucifixion of Our Lord (*Mt* 27:33-56)

FRUIT: PERSEVERANCE

Thinking of ...
Standing at the foot of the Cross beside Mary and entering into the depths of God's love for man.[1]

On Wednesday and Sunday, meditate on the "Glorious Mysteries"

First Decade: The Glorious Resurrection of Our Lord (*Jn* 20:1-29)

FRUIT: FAITH

Thinking of ...
The glorious triumph of Jesus on the third day. The empty tomb with only burial cloths. The disciple "saw and believed." (*Jn* 20:8 NAB)

Second Decade: The Ascension of Our Lord (*Lk* 24:50-53)

FRUIT: HOPE

Thinking of ...
Christ raised in glory to the right hand of the Father.[1]

Third Decade: The Descent of the Holy Spirit at Pentecost (*Acts* 2:1-41)

FRUIT: LOVE OF GOD

Thinking of ...
The Church as a family gathered together with Mary, enlivened by the powerful outpouring of the Spirit.[1] "Tongues as if fire, which parted and came to rest on each one of them." (*Acts* 2:4 NAB)

Fourth Decade: The Assumption of Mary into Heaven

FRUIT: GRACE OF A HAPPY DEATH

Thinking of ...
The Blessed Virgin Mary being escorted by angels to Heaven.

Fifth Decade: The Coronation of Mary as Queen of Heaven and Earth

FRUIT: TRUST IN THE INTERCESSION OF MARY

Thinking of ...
Crowned in glory, Mary shines forth as Queen of the Angels and Saints.[1]

[1] *Rosarium Virginis Mariae*

Acknowledgment

This book is dedicated to the Holy Trinity, Our Blessed Mother, and in gratitude for the intercession of St. John Paul II. This book was written in large part on his feast day, Oct 22, 2012. Included is a prayer by Pope John Paul II spoken at the Piazza di Spagna on December 8, 2002 the Feast of the Immaculate Conception of Mary.

> *"Holy Mary, Mother of God, pray for us!"*
> Pray, O Mother, for all of us.
> Pray for humanity who suffers poverty and injustice,
> violence and hatred, terror and war.
> Help us to contemplate with the rosary
> the mysteries of Him who "is our peace,"
> so that we will all feel involved
> in a persevering dedication of service to peace.
> Look with special attention
> upon the land in which you gave birth to Jesus,
> a land that you loved together with Him,
> and that is still so sorely tried today.
> Pray for us, Mother of hope!
> Give us days of peace, watch over our way.
> Let us see your Son as we rejoice in heaven. Amen!

More information on the Children's Rosary from:

Children's Rosary
P.O. Box 271743, West Hartford, CT 06127 USA
www.childrensrosary.org